The

HERSHEY'S KISSES™
Subtraction Book

by Jerry Pallotta
Illustrated by Rob Bolster

Cartwheel B·O·O·K·S®
SCHOLASTIC INC.

New York   Toronto   London   Auckland   Sydney   Mexico City   New Delhi   Hong Kong   Buenos Aires

Thank you to Jeannette Davis.

—— *Jerry Pallotta*

This book is dedicated to John Housley.

—— *Rob Bolster*

Text copyright © 2002 by Jerry Pallotta.
Illustrations copyright © 2002 by Rob Bolster.
All rights reserved. Published by Scholastic Inc.
SCHOLASTIC, CARTWHEEL BOOKS, and associated logos
are trademarks and/or registered trademarks of Scholastic Inc.

Library of Congress Cataloging-in-Publication Data available

ISBN 0-439-33779-8

10 9 8 7 6 5 4 3 2 1   02 03 04 05 06

Printed in the U.S.A.
This edition first printing, January 2002

In this book, you will learn

MATH IS FUN!

1 2 3 4 5 6 7 8 9 10

This is a minus sign. ——

This is an equal sign. ==

10

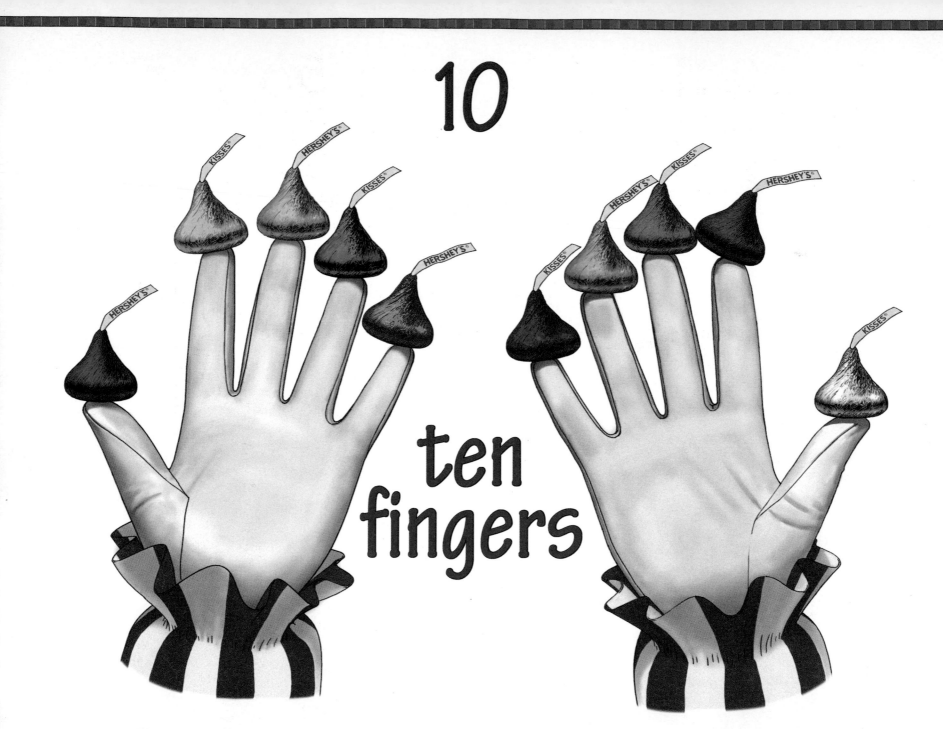

ten
fingers

This is a subtraction book. The first thing we have to do is learn
our numbers. Count the candy or count your fingers.
One, two, three, four, five, six, seven, eight, nine, ten.

ten toes

Now you can count your toes, but do it backwards. Ready, go! Ten, nine, eight, seven, six, five, four, three, two, one. Is a number missing? Yes! Zero. Zero is a number—an important number—but it has no value. There are zero pieces of candy on this page.

Subtraction is taking away something or finding a difference. Here are three beautiful paintings of HERSHEY'S KISSES® chocolates.

Look again! How many paintings are left? Three minus one equals two.
In subtraction we use a minus sign to show we are "taking away."
Three take away one equals two. Two paintings are left.

Let's start with ten this time.
Here are ten posters on a windy day.

One blew away. Ten minus one equals nine. An equation is a math sentence. The numbers on each side of the equal sign have the same value. Ten minus one has the same value as nine.

Someone has sewn a colorful nine-patch quilt with candies on it.

There has been a change. One candy has been removed. Nine minus one equals eight. The answer is eight. In subtraction we call the answer the "difference" or the "remainder."

Hooray! It's clown school graduation day! Look closely as you count the candies. They are not all the same color.

8−1=7

Eight minus one equals seven. Subtracting by one is the same as counting down. Can you see a pattern developing?

0−0=0	1−1=0	2−2=0	3−3=0	4−4=0
1−0=1	2−1=1	3−2=1	4−3=1	5−4=1
2−0=2	3−1=2	4−2=2	5−3=2	6−4=2
3−0=3	4−1=3	5−2=3	6−3=3	7−4=3
4−0=4	5−1=4	6−2=4	7−3=4	8−4=4
5−0=5	6−1=5	7−2=5	8−3=5	9−4=5
6−0=6	7−1=6	8−2=6	9−3=6	10−4=6
7−0=7	8−1=7	9−2=7	10−3=7	11−4=7
8−0=8	9−1=8	10−2=8	11−3=8	12−4=8
9−0=9	10−1=9	11−2=9	12−3=9	13−4=9

BASIC SUBTRACTION FACTS

5−5=0	6−6=0	7−7=0	8−8=0	9−9=0
6−5=1	7−6=1	8−7=1	9−8=1	10−9=1
7−5=2	8−6=2	9−7=2	10−8=2	11−9=2
8−5=3	9−6=3	10−7=3	11−8=3	12−9=3
9−5=4	10−6=4	11−7=4	12−8=4	13−9=4
10−5=5	11−6=5	12−7=5	13−8=5	14−9=5
11−5=6	12−6=6	13−7=6	14−8=6	15−9=6
12−5=7	13−6=7	14−7=7	15−8=7	16−9=7
13−5=8	14−6=8	15−7=8	16−8=8	17−9=8
14−5=9	15−6=9	16−7=9	17−8=9	18−9=9

Numbers can always be added and subtracted. It does not make sense to subtract elephants from tigers. Two tigers minus one elephant do not equal one clown. When doing subtraction, use things that are alike.

It is amazing to watch someone juggle different fruits, but you cannot subtract apples from oranges. And you will go bananas trying to subtract coconuts from cherries.

7 − 2 = 5

Seven candies were in the truck. Two fell off and are gone. That leaves five. Seven minus two equals five. If the clowns go back and pick up the two candies, there would be 5+2=7. Addition is the opposite of subtraction. Using addition, we end up back where we started.

Count the five balloons, five clouds, five birds, five mountains, five clowns, and five HERSHEY'S KISSES® chocolates.

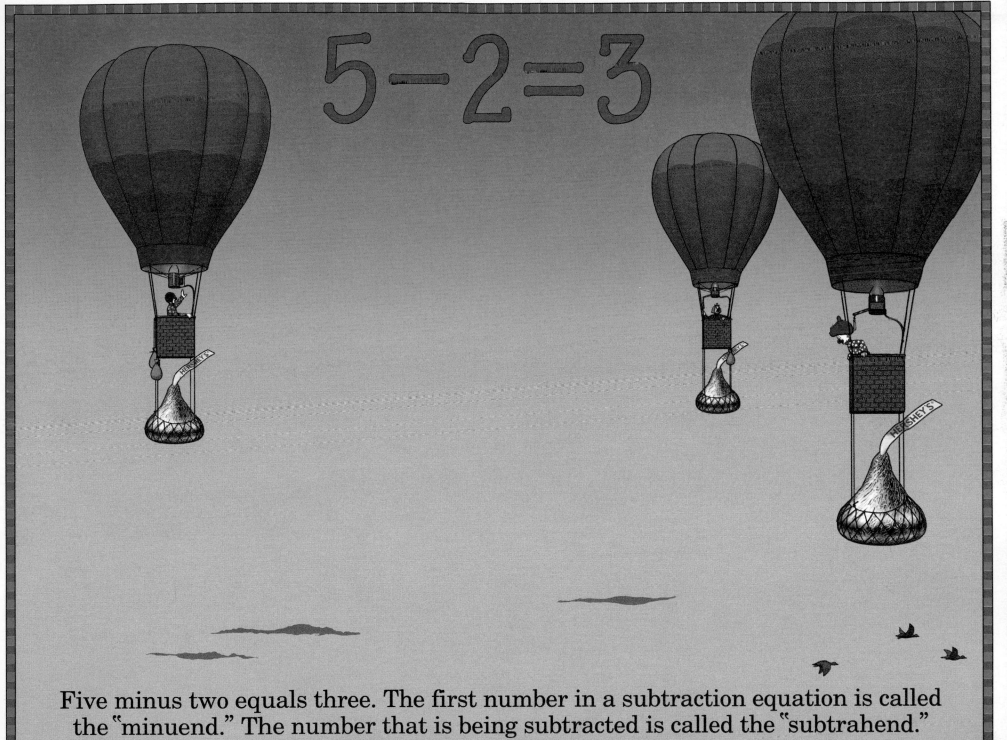

Five minus two equals three. The first number in a subtraction equation is called the "minuend." The number that is being subtracted is called the "subtrahend." Remember this—the minuend minus the subtrahend equals the difference.

Order of three coming right out!

Three minus two equals one. When doing subtraction, you cannot reverse the numbers that you are subtracting. Two minus three does not equal one.

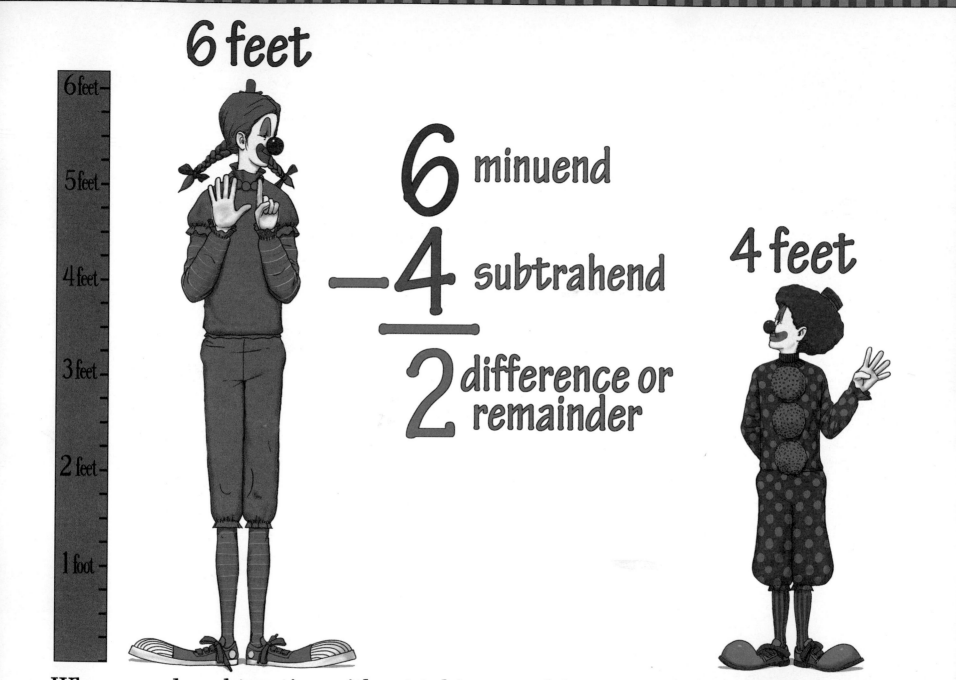

6 feet

6 minuend

− 4 subtrahend

2 difference or remainder

4 feet

6 feet —
5 feet —
4 feet —
3 feet —
2 feet —
1 foot —

When you do subtraction without taking anything away, it is called "comparison subtraction." The yellow clown is six feet tall. The blue clown is four feet tall. What is the difference in their height? Six minus four equals two. The yellow clown is two feet taller than the blue clown.

300 pounds   100 pounds

$$300 - 100 = 200$$

The green clown weighs three hundred pounds.
The striped clown weighs one hundred pounds. Here is the math: 300–100=200.
The green clown weighs two hundred pounds more than the striped clown.

We are flying through this subtraction book. This is fun!

One minus one equals zero.
There are zero HERSHEY'S KISSES on this page.
Any number minus itself is zero.

Hold on!
It's time for a ride on the roller coaster!

Here is an equation where zero is subtracted.
Four minus zero equals four.
When zero is subtracted from a number,
the value remains the same.

What would happen if you subtract more than you have? Here are ten balloons. This boy paid for twelve balloons. How many more balloons are needed?

Ten minus twelve equals negative two. The clown owes the boy two balloons. A negative number is also called a "minus number."

Here are twenty HERSHEY'S KISSES. If we make four equal groups, each group will have five. That's not subtraction! It's division! Twenty divided by four equals five. Next week we will learn division.